Churchill: Embattled Hero

Andrew Roberts

A Phoenix Paperback

This abridged edition, published in 1996 by Phoenix, contains an
abridgement of Chapter 3, The Tories Versus Churchill During the 'Finest
Hour', from *Eminent Churchillians*. Notes to this chapter appear in both
the hardback and paperback editions of the book.

First published in Great Britain by Weidenfeld & Nicolson
in 1994
A paperback edition published in 1995 by Phoenix
A division of Orion Books Ltd
Orion House, 5 Upper St Martin's Lane, London WC2H 9EA

ISBN 1 85799 533 3

Typeset by Selwood Systems, Midsomer Norton
Printed in Great Britain by Clays Ltd, St Ives Plc.

Churchill: Embattled Hero

'Seldom can a Prime Minister have taken office with the Establishment ... so dubious of the choice and so prepared to find its doubts justified,' wrote Jock Colville of Winston Churchill, adding 'within a fortnight all was changed'.

This has since become the accepted version of history, convenient both to Churchill and the Establishment. It has been presented as the story of the Conservative Party swiftly recognizing him as a national saviour and, as the Battle of Britain and the Blitz raged, quickly falling in behind him in a spirit of defiant solidarity. The truth could not have been more different.

Old men forget, but old politicians forget selectively. Many are the self-serving memoirs of Conservative MPs who prefer not to remember both the depth of the mistrust they felt for Churchill and the length of time that they continued to feel it. Such was the post-war deification of Churchill for his sublime leadership in 1940–1 that it would have been a brave Tory who told the truth about the undeclared guerrilla warfare which was fought between the new Prime Minister and the Conservative hierarchy over those fateful months. For Churchill had to employ every weapon in a Prime Minister's armoury, including one which involved changing the constitution, to establish and then press home his political advantage before he was safe.

Far from reflecting the national mood, many Conservatives in the Commons maintained a position of scepticism towards Churchill and his coalition which lasted until the summer of 1941. Criticisms, mutterings, disloyal asides and a general feeling of mistrust continued to make Churchill's leadership insecure, at least in Parliamentary terms, for far longer than is generally recognized today.

Not surprisingly, the evidence for this is somewhat patchy. People's views were changing quickly and often drastically in the highly volatile and stressful period of national peril. Because of the way Churchill's reputation stood after the war, personal reminiscences are unreliable, and only directly contemporaneous evidence is of much use. Those patrician Tory MPs who looked upon politics as a public duty rather than a career very often did not keep political diaries, especially during the period of emergency and nightly bombing. Sometimes – like the dog which did not bark in the night in the Sherlock Holmes story – it is a silence which gives the clue. The tale has therefore to be pieced together from scraps amongst hundreds of public and private sources. When it is, the picture which emerges is radically different from the accepted Tory version. The history of the period has tended to be written by the Churchillians, or at least by those sympathetic to his victorious vantage-point. It is instructive to look at it instead from the defeated Chamberlainites' point of view.

In November 1917 Churchill watched Clemenceau from the diplomatic box in the French Chamber and saw 'all around him was an assembly which would have done anything to avoid having him there, but having put him there felt they must obey'. The same may be said of Churchill and the Conservative Party in May 1940. As one of his Private Secretaries was later diplomatically to put it, 'Churchill's position in the Conservative Party was never wholly free from ambiguity, and he was conscious of it.'

After crossing the floor of the House in 1904, Churchill had soon afterwards described the Tories as the 'Party of great vested interests ... corruption at home, aggression abroad to cover it up ... sentiment by the bucketful, patriotism by the imperial pint; the open hand at the public exchequer, the open door at the public house; dear food for the millions, cheap labour for the millionaire'. They reciprocated this hostility and in 1915 their leader, Andrew Bonar Law, agreed to take the Tories into Lloyd George's coalition on the condition that Churchill was not at the Admiralty. Having, in his words, 'ratted' on the Party once, Churchill only returned to the Tory fold after Bonar Law's death. In 1931 he 're-ratted', going into the Wilderness in protest over the Party's policy on India. There he accused the Tory stalwarts, Samuel Hoare and Lord Derby, of altering evidence to a Select Committee.

Over the Abdication crisis Churchill further angered the Tory grandees. As Balfour's niece, Blanche (Baffy) Dugdale, put it in her diary: 'the possibility, amongst others, of the country being split into a King's Party versus the Government is one which fills responsible minds with anxiety'. These 'responsible people' – the Respectable Tendency of British politics – were confirmed in their view of Churchill as a maverick, but took solace from the fact that, as one Cabinet minister, Walter Elliot, put it, 'he has no support in the country, so I was in no way afraid of him'.

By the time of the Norway debate of 7 and 8 May 1940, the sense of distrust which existed on the Tory benches towards the First Lord of the Admiralty had hardly been diminished by his eight months in the War Cabinet. Despite Churchill's vigorous defence of the Chamberlain ministry in the debate, in a winding up speech which the Liberal MP, Dingle Foot, thought 'the least impressive of his career', many Tories suspected – not least because a number of Churchill's friends had gone into the 'no' lobby – that Churchill secretly wanted their leader to lose. Lord Curzon's daughter, Lady Alexandra Metcalfe, watched the debate from the Gallery and recorded seeing 'Winston, like a fat baby swinging his legs on the front bench, trying not to laugh when told by Lloyd George that the Government were using him as their air raid shelter. Stony faces on each side of him.'

One of the five backbenchers to speak up for Chamberlain in the debate, the Liberal Nationalist George Lambert, had asked: 'Who is to be Prime Minister? ... Dr Goebbels could not have done better than the House of Commons has done.' Jim Thomas believed that the Foreign Secretary, Lord Halifax, was 'favourite at the moment but I hear the usual rumour that he won't think of it. Very much persuasion is needed. Winston, of course, a runner and I have a hunch that Anthony [Eden] might step in – but this is an outside chance.'

Therefore, it was by no means certain that Churchill would be chosen, and a great shock to many Tories when he was. One of the celebrated Tennant sisters, Nancy, was married to Tommy Dugdale, Tory MP for the North Riding of Yorkshire, who had served in Baldwin's Downing Street and had also spent five years in that bastion of Chamberlainite orthodoxy, the National Government Whips' Office, before joining the Yorkshire Hussars Yeomanry in Palestine in January 1940. The letters his wife sent him give an invaluable insight into Chamberlainite Tory thinking, and her family and social connections with senior politicians gave her access to all the latest political gossip. Two days after the Prime Minister's resignation broadcast, she wrote to her husband: 'Neville spoke and spoke *so* well. I had a *real* shock at his resignation – it seemed to knock the bottom out of the home situation – I can't believe he has gone – the household was plunged into gloom as I was – and to think of Winston getting it!'

When Lady Alexandra Metcalfe, a friend of Lord Halifax's, heard on the radio that Churchill was to be Prime Minister, the news 'evoked a "Thank God" from me'. However, this was solely on the grounds that she knew Halifax did not want the job, but 'from every other point of view I think he would have been more dependable and better than Winston. One can't talk of them in the same breath and England would have had a man at the helm of whom she could have been justly proud. I am terrified of Winston, the only thing to be said is, he is preferable to L[loyd] G[eorge].'

This feeling was general amongst Conservatives. Chamberlain had won a majority of eighty-one at the Norway debate, so constitutionally he did not have to resign. But on Thursday, 9 May, he accepted the underlying logic of the Norway division and decided to go. He held a meeting with Churchill and Halifax at 4.30 p.m., which ascertained that Churchill would succeed. When the news came through on the morning of 10 May that Hitler had attacked in the West, Chamberlain attempted to countermand this. The key man in forcing him out seems to have been the diminutive Lord Privy Seal, Sir Kingsley Wood, who made it clear at Cabinet that he could not use the new military situation to change his mind. Wood had been in contact with Churchill since the debate and suspicious Chamberlainites saw his subsequent appointment as Chancellor of the Exchequer by Churchill as a reward for changing sides.

More extraordinary for Chamberlainites than their hero's fall was that their former arch-enemy, Winston Churchill, should have won the crown he had been so long suspected of coveting. 'I could hardly control myself,' wrote Nancy Dugdale. 'Everyone here, Lady C[urzon]-H[owe], etc., will *hate* it and the country people also. They say "we never thought of him, Lord Halifax, yes, but Mr Churchill, never". First they never thought Neville would go as the debate meant nothing to them and they still have complete confidence in him.'

As Nancy Dugdale's letter to her husband continued:

W.C. they regard with complete mistrust as you know, and they hate his boasting broadcasts. W.C. is really the counterpart of Goering in England, full of the desire for blood, 'Blitzkrieg' and bloated with ego and over-feeding, the same treachery running through his veins, punctuated by heroics and hot air. I can't tell you how depressed I feel about it.

This negative attitude towards Churchill's wartime broadcasts may sound surprising today, but from political cognoscenti who were familiar with, if not immune to, his rhetoric, there were constant criticisms. After his broadcast to the neutrals of January 1940, Lady Alexandra Metcalfe had written in her diary: 'It is incredible that a man in his position should make such gaffes. His bragging about the war at sea is followed every time by some appalling loss, last time two destroyers, and his voice oozes with port, brandy and the chewed cigar.'

Churchill's undisguised fascination with warfare was considered somewhat bad form by many Tory MPs, a large number of whom had served in the First World War. Ninety per cent of those Tory knights of the shire over forty-five who represented safe seats voted for Chamberlain. This was the Conservative Party's backbone and they proved some of the most intractable Churchill-sceptics.

Despite their reluctance to vote for him in the Norway division, many of the abstainers, non-attenders and even some rebels were nevertheless still devoted to Chamberlain personally. The high drama of the debate helped induce a 7 feeling of bitterness against the rebels, which took months to subside. A typical example was the taunt of the Chamberlainite loyalist, Kenneth Pickthorn, at the young rebel, Richard Law, son of the former Conservative Prime Minister, who was leaving the Chamber after the debate: 'Well, I expect you'll get your reward!' His suspicions seemed to be confirmed when Law received a ministerial post at the War Office soon afterwards.

When the House met on 13 May, after the Whitsun recess, a Chamberlainite backlash was well underway. William Spens, Chairman of the Tory backbenchers' 1922 committee, told the arch-Chamberlainite Under-Secretary at the Foreign Office, Rab Butler, that 'three-quarters' of Tory MPs were 'ready to put Chamberlain back'. A number had come under severe pressure from their constituencies to support Chamberlain.

Many people thought that the rebels acted as they had from self-serving or egotistical motives. The Whips' nickname for the anti-appeasement group around Eden was 'Glamour Boys'. As Tory MP Victor Raikes wrote to a fellow Chamberlainite loyalist, Alan Lennox-Boyd, on 10 May, 'The new political orientation rather depresses me…. Anyway the late Prime Minister's critics are doing well out of it, so some people should be pleased.' The impression quickly got around that the new Government, as Raikes put it, 'is in fact … deliberately composed of anti-Munichites'. However, this was far from the truth, as two-thirds of Chamberlain's ministers were reappointed by Churchill and only twelve senior posts went to newcomers. Nevertheless, the sense of betrayal amongst Chamberlainites was acute.

A recurring theme in the hundreds of letters which Chamberlain received after his resignation was that the game was by no means over. Rab Butler wrote: 'I hope you will always realise the strength and number of your friends and how much we count on your presence in the Government.' Chamberlain was still Leader of the Party, and Butler feared that 'times will come when I and my friends will need these great qualities of yours ... whatever the future might bring and wherever your influence may be required.' It was not the letter of a man who had given up all hope of his master returning. He was articulating the views of many Chamberlainites when, in a subtle critique of Churchill's friends and confidants, he added: 'There are certain virtues and values which those of us, who have been associated with authority since 1931, hold dear, which we are sure you will perpetuate.'

The sense of dozens of such letters of support for Chamberlain is best summed up by that from the back-bencher Captain Edward Cobb: 'The fact that you were prepared to serve the new P.M. resolves the doubts of a good many of us who had been doubtful of whether we would like to receive the Whip in these circumstances. If he is good enough for you he must be good enough for us.' One MP, Patrick Donner, wrote to say that, 'if we lose altogether the only leader we have – and there is no other – the standards of value in the party will disappear and with them the reason for continuance'. Sir Archibald Geddes wrote, 'So far I have met no-one in the Regiment who would like to see Winston PM.'

Walter Liddall, who had set up a 'Loyalty to Leader' group in the Parliamentary Party, wrote to assure Chamberlain that every member of it would support him 'not for a day or month, but always'. This turned out to be no exaggeration. John Moore-Brabazon told Samuel Hoare, 'this is *not* the last war administration by a long way'. He was wrong, but these were not the sentiments of men who had totally reconciled themselves to the new regime. Many were afraid that their political careers would be stymied by Churchill taking revenge for the catcalls and humiliations to which various Tories had subjected him during the Wilderness Years. The first manifestation of the Chamberlainites' unaltered loyalties came on 13 May, when only the Labour benches applauded Churchill's first entry into the Chamber as Prime Minister. Loud and prolonged Tory cheers greeted Chamberlain when he took his seat on the Front Bench next to the new Prime Minister.

The Chamberlainites' sense of scepticism and resentment against Churchill, which was to metamorphosize into support and eventually devotion, is fully documented in the newly-discovered diary of Captain Charles Waterhouse. 'A true blue Tory, a country gentleman, a Life Guard in the First World War', Waterhouse had been MP for South-East Leicester since 1924. A Derbyshire landowner, Great War MC, Deputy-Lieutenant of the county and Justice of the Peace, Waterhouse was the epitome of the traditional shire Tory. He had been a Whip since 1935 and, after the outbreak of war, was appointed

Assistant Postmaster-General. The significance of his diary lies in the extent to which it reflects the views of mainstream Conservatives as they gradually reconciled themselves to Churchill. Waterhouse was a close friend of the Chief and Deputy Chief Whips, David Margesson and James Stuart, and nobody could better personify the Conservative Party as it was cajoled, persuaded, bribed and charmed into eventual support for the new Prime Minister.

Waterhouse's attitude towards the Norway debate was characteristically forthright. Written at 1.45 a.m., on his return from the Commons to his flat in Lowndes Square, he recorded:

> Division 281 against 200 with I estimate 45 of our wettest voting with the Opposition – the usual crowd of Anglo-American – general disgruntled – sacked – aspirant – Glamour, with a few well-meaning sentimentalists and amateur strategists thrown in.... I do not see that [Chamberlain] has any course but resignation. He cannot stand the strain of war against half the world, two Opposition parties and a considerable section of his own. Hitler will thank Thor for our quislings.

The language of treachery – 'quislings', 'fifth columnists', etc. – was freely used by the Chamberlainites in describing the Norway rebels. One of them, Maurice Hely-Hutchinson, told the Norway rebel, Somerset de Chair, that his friends were like 'parachutist troops who had descended behind the lines in Conservative uniform'.

Waterhouse wound up his diary entry on that momentous night:

> We gave the PM a great reception when he left the House after the division but all this is clearly having an effect on him. W.C. after his bloody-mindedness of a fortnight ago seems definitely to have changed his fickle mind and tonight put in heavy blows in defence of the Government position.

The 'bloody-mindedness' reference was probably to Churchill's recent demand for a greater say in the running of the war. Having originally intended to go for four days' fishing at Kelso over Whitsun with his neighbour Lord Belper, the political situation meant that Waterhouse had reluctantly to be in London on Saturday, 11 May.

Waterhouse wrote when he got back:

> Neville Chamberlain announced on the 9 p.m. wireless that as the Socialists had refused to serve under him he had agreed to serve under Winston Churchill. If ever there was a mark of real greatness it is this ... the PM is prepared for the nation's sake to serve under one who until lately – very lately – was first an open opponent and then a possibly not over-loyal colleague. So be it.

This was a suspicion many MPs had about the new Prime Minister. Despite his conspicuously vigorous defence of the Government in the debate, when some assumed his own career may also have been on the line, Chamberlainites wondered whether Churchill had been working behind the scenes to make himself Prime Minister. He had not intrigued, unless taking advice from Kingsley Wood not to bow to pressure from those who wanted Halifax can be counted. Churchill reacted angrily against even his closest friends who gloated too publicly at Chamberlain's downfall, and was zealous in observing all the proprieties towards his predecessor.

Waterhouse's estimation of the new Prime Minister was typical:

> Winston has his ambition and thank God Chamberlain is there to keep the country straight. I do not think that W.C. will be comfortable as leader, his mind is essentially critical and volcanic and he is used to proposing and propounding schemes and ideas and for having these schemes critically examined and as a rule gracefully withdrawing them. Such is not the role of a PM.

Lord Halifax echoed these misgivings, writing to Lady Alexandra Metcalfe from his suite in the Dorchester on 13 May: 'I don't think WSC will be a very good PM though I think the country will think he gives them a fillip.'

It was to the composition of Churchill's coalition that Tories immediately addressed themselves, in a mood to have their anxieties and suspicions confirmed. 'As always must happen after such an upheaval he will from group loyalty have to give office to a considerable number of people such as Bob Boothby who have brains but lack character and, in that particular case, decency,' assumed Waterhouse. This also worried Nancy Dugdale, who warned her husband: 'Now all those reptile satellites – Duff Cooper – Bob Boothby – Brendan Bracken, etc. – will ooze into jobs they are utterly unfitted for. All we are fighting to uphold will go out of public life. I regard this as a greater disaster than the invasion of the Low Countries.' That, she considered, was merely 'the inevitable unrolling of "Mein Kampf"'.

References to standards of public life were a common theme amongst Chamberlainites. They considered that what Butler had called their 'virtues and values' were under threat from the Churchillian and 'Glamour Boy' adventurers, who supposedly had lower standards of political decency. 'The crooks are on top as they were in the last war,' wrote Baldwin's confidant, Lord Davidson. 'We must keep our powder dry!' Halifax also believed that 'the gangsters will shortly be in complete control'. Churchill's friends, associates and fellow anti-appeasers of the Wilderness Years were cordially detested by the Tory knights.

As well as Duff Cooper, the only minister to resign over Munich; Brendan Bracken, Churchill's widely distrusted right-hand man, whose murky Irish background made Tories suspicious; and Robert Boothby, the flamboyant free-thinking anti-appeaser; there was Churchill's son-in-law, Duncan Sandys, whose use of leaked information over rearmament had infuriated the Party; and most of all the press magnate, Lord Beaverbrook, whom Tories disliked as a thrusting colonial. They had decried the anti-Baldwin campaigns of arguably the most powerful popular newspaper in the history of Fleet Street. All of these friends of Churchill aroused the ire of the Respectable Tendency, who dreaded their entry into the Government.

The formation of Churchill's coalition in the week after 10 May 1940 was a delicate juggling act carried out with great dexterity. The spoils were divided in such a way as to leave every group, if not content, at least unable to complain overmuch. Most important for Churchill's survival, it accorded the Chamberlainites just enough senior places to remove their immediate discontent, yet not enough to give them overall control of the ministry. The linchpin in its formation, as with so much in politics since 1931, was the Government Chief Whip, Captain David Margesson. He had first joined the Whips' Office in 1924, becoming its Chief in November 1931. He more than deserved his reputation as the toughest Chief Whip in British political history. Tall, gaunt and a keen huntsman, Margesson was the grandson of Lord Buckingham and the Respectable Tendency's sergeant-major.

Guilty Men, the left-wing journalists' polemic against the Chamberlainites which was published in July 1940, explained how Margesson would isolate rebels: 'If the cad won't play the game, well he must be sent to Coventry. The other fellows shun and spurn him.' Churchill well knew the treatment; Margesson's period of primacy during the MacDonald, Baldwin and Chamberlain Premierships coincided exactly with Churchill's Wilderness Years. 'His task was to keep the Conservative dissidents isolated,' says a leading historian of the period, 'to put them under constant pressure from the party organisations in their constituencies, to divert patronage away 15 from them, and to make sure their ostracism by the bulk of the party was as complete as he could make it.'

In mid-1939 the Whips plotted to have Churchill deselected before the general election which had to be called before June 1940. As Jim Thomas wrote to 'Bobbety' Cranborne that summer, after Lord Camrose's failed *Daily Telegraph* campaign to get Churchill into the Cabinet:

The Whips are hopeless, hopeless, hopeless and Tommy [Dugdale] the worst. He said to me yesterday that the increased [vote] at Caerphilly [by-election] had knocked Camrose on the head and that it showed the PM's popularity and now all could be prepared for the General Election next October. I said what about the war next week? But he said that the only thing that would make war certain would be Winston in the Cabinet. Managed to keep my temper....

Three days before the Norway debate, Thomas wrote to Cranborne, who was ill, reporting how 'the Whips were endeavouring to throw the responsibility [for the Norway campaign] on Winston, but they eventually thought it wiser to make use of him'. At the meeting to decide whether Halifax or Churchill should succeed him, Margesson said that 'he found a growing feeling in the Labour Party' of opposition to having a Prime Minister from the House of Lords. This information may have helped ease Churchill into the pole position Halifax had left open for him.

The senior government posts largely chose themselves. Labour took two places in the War Cabinet with the

Party's Leader and Deputy Leader, Clement Attlee and Arthur Greenwood, becoming Ministers without Portfolio. Having been vetoed by Labour for the posts of Chancellor of the Exchequer or Leader of the House, Chamberlain became Lord President of the Council. Halifax stayed on as Foreign Secretary and Churchill became Minister of Defence as well as Prime Minister. The only senior Chamberlainite to be dismissed altogether was Hoare, who considered himself very hard done by. He begged Churchill for the Viceroyalty of India, but was in the end fobbed off with the Madrid Embassy. He then immediately began haggling for an extra £2,000 in special allowances, coincidentally the same sum he was secretly receiving annually from Beaverbrook for political services rendered.

It is a sign of Churchill's perceived weakness that Sir John Simon, the Tweedledum of appeasement to Hoare's Tweedledee, was allowed to become Lord Chancellor. It helped that he was the leader of the small National Liberal Party. On the second day of the Norway debate Lord Dunglass had offered to sacrifice both Simon and Hoare to propitiate Tory malcontents. Despite this, Simon was given the Woolsack by Churchill and spent the rest of the war performing worthy tasks such as chairing a royal commission on the birth rate and passing legal reforms on frustrated contracts.

Only one of Chamberlain's ministers actually refused to serve under Churchill. Oliver Stanley was the son of the Lord Derby whom the new Prime Minister had accused of cheating during the Indian constitutional struggle. He had become War Minister after Hore-Belisha was sacked in January 1940. But having clashed repeatedly with Churchill, his naval opposite number, during the Phoney War, he felt, as he told fellow Tory MP Victor Cazalet on 21 May, 'that my personal relations with the new Prime Minister were such that it would not have been honest of me to take the job which was offered me'. Two days later he wrote to Chamberlain: 'I only hope that the country will not have to pay a terrible penalty for the mistake it made,' adding, as did so many of Chamberlain's correspondents: 'I hope some day I may be serving under you again.'

Stanley told Halifax, 'The principal ground being that he could not serve Winston loyally having seen so much of him in the last two months. It would never work.' Nevertheless, Halifax 'exhorted him a good deal and made him promise to see Neville before seeing Winston. This he did, but to my surprise when I saw Neville in the evening he told me that he also had concurred with Oliver on the whole, his reasons being that Oliver would be able to steady the boat in the House of Commons from outside. So that is that.'

After being reappointed, Sir John Reith wrote in his diary: 'how filthy this treatment – and what a rotten government.... A dirty business every way.' The staunchly Chamberlainite editor of *The Times*, Geoffrey Dawson, sarcastically recorded the appointment of 'colourful Kingsley Wood' to the Exchequer and commented on the jobs for Leo Amery at the India Office, Duff Cooper at the Ministry of Information and Lord Lloyd at Colonies:

'too many friends!' Geoffrey Shakespeare, a National Liberal MP, wrote to his party leader, Simon: 'We all feel deeply that the new government ... necessary as it may be to secure the co-operation of Labour – should have been launched on a wave of pettiness and spite.' For Nancy Dugdale the appointments of Wood, Duff Cooper and Churchill's old friend, the Liberal leader Sir Archibald Sinclair, to the Air Ministry, 'makes me sick'. She was not alone amongst Chamberlainites in blaming Margesson for bringing the 'W.C. element into public life.... I can't bear to think of Winston's overweening ambition being satisfied.'

Chamberlain's former Minister for the Co-ordination of Defence, Lord Chatfield, told Hoare: 'Winston seems indeed to have challenged fate by the selection of some of his colleagues. I am really glad I am out of the picture and only a faraway memory. You will soon be in harness again'. Halifax recorded Victor Cazalet's 'horror at the appointment of Beaverbrook to look after the production of aircraft'. The Chamberlainite minister, Euan Wallace, put Duff Cooper's inclusion in the Government solely down to his wife, the famous socialite beauty Lady Diana. Halifax gave Churchill little credit for having to construct a government in the middle of a blitzkrieg:

Apart from the merits of his appointments he seems to me to have been incredibly rough in his method of handling those he was going to drop! Merely a message through his secretary! And in two cases at least that I know, the person concerned first saw it in the paper and heard it on the wireless. I think even in war things should be done differently to that. He's an odd creature.

Churchill made vigorous use of the Honours system in attempting to drum up support for his Government, remove awkward customers and create vacancies in the Commons. Bracken was under no illusions as to the power which control over the Honours system could give the executive and he made sure that people knew how closely he, as PPS to the Prime Minister, was personally involved in the decision-making process. 'When MPs wished to indicate that they had suffered a change of heart since the days when Mr Chamberlain had been their only true prophet and Mr Churchill a noisy brawler kicking up an ungentlemanly fuss in the political wastelands which were his proper home', it was to Bracken that they had to make their supplications.

For the moment, however, that was not happening. When the question arose of Churchill taking over the Leadership of the Party from Chamberlain, he was shrewd enough to eschew it, writing to Chamberlain on 16 May: 'I am, of course, a Conservative. But, as Prime Minister of a National government formed on the widest basis, and comprising the three parties, I feel that it would be better for me not to undertake the Leadership of any one political party.' He made great efforts not to antagonize the man whom the majority of by far the largest party in the Commons still saw as their spiritual, as well as titular, leader.

'During the early days of his premiership', recalled the

civil servant Lawrence Burgis about the War Cabinet meetings he attended, 'one thing struck me most forceably and that was the courtesy and deference with which Churchill treated Neville Chamberlain.' This he ascribed to Churchill's 'capacity really to forgive and really to forget', but it might just as convincingly be put down to sensible politics. As Lloyd George's secretary put it more starkly in mid-June 1940, 'The plain fact is that Winston is afraid of Chamberlain'. Good manners, as the matronly saying goes, cost nothing; but snubbing Chamberlain in the six months after he took office might have cost Churchill his Premiership.

In 1966 a well-informed but anonymous correspondent wrote to *The Times* correcting the sentence in Margesson's obituary which stated that Churchill had been 'magnanimous' in reappointing the Chief Whip. 'In the early days it was the unswerving allegiance of Chamberlain and Margesson which rallied the Conservatives in the House of Commons behind [Churchill]. Had he begun by dismissing the Chief Whip the support he in fact received would have been much less readily given.' Considering that some Tories wrote to Chamberlain after the Norway debate to say how reluctant they were to take the Churchill Government's Whip, this was no exaggeration.

For Churchill a potentially dangerous myth was emerging amongst Chamberlainites who questioned his loyalty during the Phoney War. As Waterhouse noted on 12 May, 'Cabinet making is going full blast – there is every appearance to those closest up that much thought has been given and not a few preliminary arrangements made in advance.'

For him, as for so many of the Respectable Tendency, the ultimate bogeyman was Lord Beaverbrook. This Canadian adventurer personified everything they disliked and distrusted in politics. He had opposed their hero Stanley Baldwin throughout the 1930s and, despite having been a keen appeaser, was just the sort of dynamic outsider whom they could be relied upon to despise and even fear.

> The exact fitting of the puzzle matters little [wrote Waterhouse]; what does matter terribly is that behind and through the whole issue is a sinister little figure ... who will I believe eventually figure in the administration. If one sells one's soul to the devil one must at some time pay the price, but it is hard to make the country share in the outlay.

The mood in the Whips' Office was equally wary of the new regime. According to Waterhouse's diary, the Deputy Chief Whip, James Stuart, 'views the whole box of tricks with the greatest possible misgiving and will get out of the Whips' Office if he can. He has already written at length to Chamberlain but David Margesson very naturally wants him to stop in.' Waterhouse himself daily expected the sack: 'I ... have been interested in my departmental work and shall be very sorry to leave it but politically it will be much better to watch this racket from the outside.'

Nancy Dugdale felt much the same about her husband, writing to him on 15 May:

> For the first time I have felt glad for you that you have shaken the dust of politics off your feet. Beaverbrook,

Duff Cooper – Rob Hudson as Minister of Agriculture ... I'm just waiting for the 9 p.m. news to hear Bob Boothby has got a job to bring up the rear of reptiles ... 9.30 – I knew it! He has an Under-Secretaryship! And Harold Macmillan ... War always throws up the dregs.... Really Harold Macmillan and Bob Boothby as bedfellows is a new one on me!

Her husband would doubtless have picked up the reference to Macmillan's wife, who was also Boothby's mistress, which would have been missed by army censors. However, the concluding sentence of her letter permitted no misinterpretation: 'I suppose one must hide one's loathing although it is very hard to do.'

Far from instilling a spirit of unity, the military reverses on the Continent provided fresh fuel for the Chamberlainites' invective, little realizing at the beginning that they would be blamed. After reading how Rotterdam had fallen to fifth columnists and parachutists, and that the Germans had crossed the River Maas at Maastricht, Waterhouse allowed himself a dig against Churchill: 'I hope the new P.M. in his effort to fix up his friends at home will not for long neglect his enemies abroad.' As for the reason for Chamberlain's fall:

Norway, having served its purpose, is now forgotten. The *Express* yesterday referred to it as an 'incident' and the 'wisdom' of our withdrawal has been commented on. When this business is all fixed it will be instructive to re-read the Hansards of Tuesday and Wednesday [the Norway debate] and note the number of things said by the various quislings which they will shortly wish had never passed their lips.

Waterhouse also noted how many MPs came up to him in the Smoking Room to apologize for their behaviour during the Norway debate: 'People who voted against [Chamberlain] on Wednesday are endeavouring to explain their vote away.' Many had not expected to bring down the Government.

Back in the Smoking Room the Chamberlainite reaction against Margesson was well under way. Five senior back-benchers – Robert Smith, Hon. Ralph Beaumont, Edward Cobb, the former PPS to Oliver Stanley, John Crowder and Alexander Erskine-Hill, a senior member of the 1922 Executive – told Waterhouse that 'they thought David had passed his time of usefulness'. Among the criticisms levelled at him was that he was 'out of touch' and had 'gone over to Winston'. Waterhouse duly reported this whispering campaign against their Chief to the Whips' Office.

'I hope Winston won't lead us into anything too rash,' wrote Halifax's son, Charles Wood, MP for York, from Palestine; 'I can't really see what difference except perhaps psychologically the new Government will make.' He echoed the by then prevailing view: 'They seemed to have behaved shamefully in the House of Commons.' John Colville, Erskine-Hill's father-in-law and Chamberlain's Scottish Secretary (who was not reappointed to Churchill's Government), complained to his wife that Churchill was 'no gentleman'.

When Churchill appointed a friend, Harcourt Johnstone, to the Government, he managed to hurt the *amour propre* of the Liberals. Their Chief Whip, Sir Percy Harris, recorded in his memoirs that, 'What was resented by my colleagues was not so much that they had not been included, but that it had been thought necessary to go outside to fill a ministerial post.' Johnstone was appointed Minister of Overseas Trade without being either a business expert or even an MP, although he was a Liberal. Tall, Whiggish and elegant, 'Crinks' Johnstone was 'reputed to have more waistcoats than anyone else'. A legendary *bon vivant*, he allegedly died from over-eating.

Johnstone was not appreciated by the more hard-nosed Chamberlainites. When he was eventually elected to Parliament unopposed and took his seat in the Commons, there was not a murmur of support from any Member. 'I never remember such an entry,' wrote Waterhouse. 'Winston was there to see the advent of his personally selected tame member.' In the debates which followed, as Harris related with some satisfaction, 'the younger Tories took pleasure in ragging him and asking him awkward questions'. The explanation for his appointment was simply that like Lord Sherwood and James de Rothschild, who also at different times became ministers, Churchill enjoyed their company, as was witnessed by their membership of The Other Club.

Contrary to Jock Colville's claim, by late May the Tory Establishment was no more reconciled to the new Government than they had been a fortnight before. Robert Bruce Lockhart, who used to write 'Londoners' Diary' for

Beaverbrook's *Evening Standard* but was then working in the Political Intelligence Department of the Foreign Office, noted in his diary how, on 21 May, the Manchester Tory MP and former captain of Lancashire County Cricket Club, Peter Eckersley, 'who is anti-Winston', told him that the 'revolt was a farce and will do no good. Winston won't last five months! Opposition from Tories is already beginning.'

'Yesterday the House was as breezy as a girls' school,' wrote Waterhouse on 22 May. ' "All is lost" sort of attitude in evidence in many quarters.'

On 23 May Richard Law wrote to his fellow Norway rebel Lord Wolmer:

> My impression from the very outside fringe of things is that the new Government – or rather the new elements in it – are fighting a war on two fronts, against Hitler and against enemies much nearer home. I did not like the House yesterday at all. I wish Winston weren't such a child in these matters.

Nancy Dugdale agreed about the coalition's difficulties. 'As to the Government,' she wrote to Tommy on 24 May, 'nobody I have talked to likes it ... they hate "the wild man" and don't trust him. They are for the first time really concerned about the War. Those who know think the Government beyond words.'

The end of May and the first days of June saw the miracle of the BEF's evacuation from Dunkirk. According to one historian of the coalition, 'The backing of many Tory MPs was conditional upon there being no direct clash of loyalty involving the Party Leader.... Dunkirk, we must conclude, was a deliverance for Churchill as it was for the British nation.' The sense of relief that the army was back safely soon turned into a hunt for scapegoats. Chamberlain and the 'Old Gang' proved ideal targets, and they were blamed for the defeat. Their unpopularity was stoked by the bestseller *Guilty Men*, co-written by three Beaverbrook journalists including Michael Foot. Combined with the concurrent surge in Churchill's popularity, this evaporation of public support for Chamberlain proved more than anything else the spur for uncommitted Tories to switch allegiances away from the Chamberlainites. However, the rearguard action fought by the Chamberlainite rump was far longer, tougher and more bitter than is now supposed.

Ambitious MPs concerned about their careers did not miss the signs of the Prime Minister's hugely increased popularity after Dunkirk. One Chamberlainite, Sir Frank Sanderson – who had the *savoir-faire* to keep old press cuttings with headlines like 'Sir Frank Says Hitler's Policy is One of Peace' – addressed the annual dinner of the Ealing Primrose League on 1 June 1940. 'There is not a more loyal man in this country than myself in regard to the late Prime Minister and still leader of our Party – Neville Chamberlain,' he said, to two apologetic little claps from a lady and gentleman in the back row as the rest of the audience sat in silence. After a moment he continued: 'But there comes a time when a specialist brain must needs fill a special position.' At this reference to Churchill, recorded the *Middlesex County Times*, Ealing

Town Hall erupted into loud and prolonged applause. Conservative MPs could not but appreciate the implications of this and hundreds of similar manifestations of the national change of mood.

On 4 June, the Dunkirk evacuation completed, Churchill delivered his sublime 'We shall fight on the beaches' speech to the House of Commons. There were complaints. France was still in the war, if only for another fortnight, and his veiled references to her possible surrender worried MPs. In the House, Euan Wallace noted that 'there was some controversy in the Smoking Room afterwards about his double reference to fighting alone'. Cecil King of the *Daily Mirror* quoted from his diary for 4 June how Lloyd George had told him 'Churchill's reception in the House was very half-hearted, he got far less applause than was usually accorded to Chamberlain in spite of his magnificent speech'. The Tories were still refusing to give their wholehearted support despite the gravity of the situation and the glory of his oratory. Indeed, for some, the more magnificent his rhetoric, the more suspicious they became. This was not confined to the politicians. On 16 May 1940 Colville had recorded how his fellow No. 10 Private Secretaries had said of a message from Churchill that it was just 'blasted rhetoric.... He is still thinking of his books.'

On 5 June, after Duff Cooper had experienced a particularly tough time at the despatch box, Wallace recorded Walter Elliot's conclusion that the coalition's 'honeymoon is coming to an end'. In fact, the heat was now being turned up on Chamberlain. Writing to his sisters, Ida and

Hilda, Chamberlain referred to 'a party meeting every evening at the Reform Club under the chairmanship of Clement Davies, that treacherous Welshman'. Amery, Macmillan and Boothby sometimes attended in order to orchestrate Chamberlain's removal from office. But Churchill would have none of it, telling Chamberlain somewhat hyperbolically that 'we had gone in together and would if necessary go down together'.

Churchill knew the Parliamentary mathematics remained unaltered whatever happened to Chamberlain's reputation outside Parliament. The Conservatives had won a landslide victory in the 1935 general election, and as the political truce called at the outbreak of war prohibited any contested by-elections by the major parties, they enjoyed an automatic in-built preponderance for the rest of the war. Churchill had no real option but to stand by Chamberlain, the ultimate guarantor of his Premiership. Their personal relationship was developing well, and Churchill entrusted his predecessor with ever more important tasks on the Home Front, which he knew would be carried out with loyalty and thoroughness.

Cecil King believed that 'time and the Nation are so clearly against the Tory backbenchers that Churchill can defy them and get away with it'. But the Prime Minister himself could not risk it. A lifetime in politics had taught him how fickle public opinion could be. Churchill exerted himself and managed to stop the anti-Chamberlain press pogrom almost overnight.

On 7 June Churchill told King:

The men who had supported Chamberlain and hounded [him] were still MPs. Chamberlain had got the biggest cheer when they met the House after forming the War Administration. A General Election is not possible during a War and so the present House of Commons, however unrepresentative of feeling in the country, had to be reckoned with as the ultimate source of power for the duration. If Churchill trampled on these men, as he could trample on them, they would set themselves against him and in such internecine strife lay the Germans' best chance of victory.

He would 'not run a Government of revenge', knowing that anyhow 'they were everywhere, not only in the political world, but among the fighting Service Chiefs and the Civil Service chiefs. To clean all these out would be a task impossible in the disastrous state in which we find ourselves.'

By 14 June the Germans were in Paris, and two days later Marshal Pétain replaced Paul Reynaud as French Prime Minister and began to sue for peace. On 18 June Churchill made his 'Finest Hour' speech. One might have assumed that this was the moment when all British politicians would bury their hatchets and fall in behind him, but still the doubts and mutterings continued. The Labour Minister for Economic Warfare, Hugh Dalton, noted after the speech: 'It is noticeable how he is much more loudly cheered by the Labour Party than by the general body of Tory supporters. The relative silence of these latter is regarded by some as "sinister".'

Dalton asked his PPS, John Wilmot, to ascertain Chamberlainite opinion and heard that 'many Tories feel the Labour Party has much too large a share, both in offices and the determination of Government policy'. Dalton thought that 'there is some danger in this situation and it must be watched. One very obvious conclusion is that we must not push the Old Man [Chamberlain] out of the Government. For he would then become a centre of disaffection and a rallying-point for real opposition.' Dalton thought that it was better to 'leave him where he is, as a decaying hostage'.

Waterhouse commented on the 'Finest Hour' speech: 'He was not in his best form. He was inclined to be hesitant to start with and introduced some rather cheap jibes and jeers which seemed to me ill-suited to the gravity of the moment.' Writing to her husband the same day, Nancy Dugdale reported a conversation she had had with Lord Dunglass and the Whip, Patrick Munro, at Prunier's Restaurant: 'Alec said in the last fortnight, and indeed since W came in, the H of C had stunk in the nostrils of the decent people. The kind of people surrounding W are the scum and the peak came when Brendan was made a PC! For what services rendered heaven knows.' Dunglass told Nancy how 'the lobbying against Neville is terrific', but 'that was stopped'. He added that

they are endeavouring to keep a remnant of cleanliness in public life. Jim Thomas has joined them in the Whips office and he's being quite good so far. Pat said in reply to my asking what he thought of the Government and

David M who has most undoubtedly served God and Mammon with equal ease, Pat said that they just *never* allow themselves to think about it.

She confirmed that Lady Wilson had told her that Sir Horace was 'always getting ill-mannered messages from WC to the effect that he is only to do what he is told and to keep his place etc.'. Both Wilson (who was godfather to the Dugdales' son) and Dunglass told her 'that W.C. consults N.C. about *nothing*, neither the small or large things and he tells him nothing'. She concluded by relating an incident when the week before Duff Cooper had got 'really *very* drunk indeed' and had 'hissed hate and was *awful* … the night after Italy came into the War and he delivered his shameful and outrageously stupid broadcast, I felt ashamed to be English'.

The (quite unfounded) criticism of Churchill for not consulting Chamberlain enough was echoed by Halifax, who, walking to the Foreign Office with Victor Cazalet in early June, complained that the Prime Minister 'is getting very arrogant and hates criticism of any kind … it is almost impossible to get five minutes conversation with him'.

Churchill was fully conscious of the way many backbenchers still felt, and at the end of his speech-notes for the secret session on 20 June he confronted it head on. 'Lastly, say a word about ourselves,' they read. 'How the new Government was formed. Tell the story Chamberlain's actions. Imperative there should be loyalty, union among men who have joined hands. Otherwise no means of standing the shocks and strains which are coming. I have a right to depend loyalty to the Administration and feel we have only one enemy to face.' This was probably a reference to the continued attacks on Chamberlain.

On 22 June Vichy France signed an armistice with Germany, the terms of which arrived in London two days later, to general consternation. Again, instead of forging national cohesion, it encouraged a renewed offensive to force Chamberlain from office.

On 2 July Waterhouse wrote: 'The House of Commons is a hell of a place. No one intends to be defeatist but a more lugubrious lot of blighters it would be hard to find. With a few examples, among whom Jock Erskine stands out, everyone gives the impression that things are so damned bad we will be lucky if we survive.' Dining with Margesson and Stuart he heard that 'folk are not pleased about the evacuation of the Channel Islands. Much comment on the "fight on the beaches, fight on the shores" speech.' So even that, the most memorable of all the Churchillian wartime orations, was criticized at the time by Tory backbenchers. Waterhouse was soon complaining that 'the Channel Islands evacuation does not seem to have been a British Epic'.

When, on 30 June, Leo Amery and Randolph Churchill expressed the view that Chamberlain 'ought to be punished', the Prime Minister answered: 'We don't want to punish anybody – except the enemy.' Chamberlain owed his successor a debt for this support, and he resolved to pay it. At the end of June the political correspondent of the *Financial News*, Paul Einzig, wrote to Chamberlain to complain about the lack of support his followers were giving the Prime Minister. As he later wrote in his memoirs:

> For nearly two months after the advent of Churchill the overwhelming majority of Tory backbenchers, whatever their inner feelings may have been, gave no outward evidence of their support for him. Indeed on many occasions they went out of their way to demonstrate their unwillingness to do so. There was strong resentment amongst them over the appointment of some Tory 'rebels' – looked upon as 'traitors' by orthodox Tories – to Ministerial posts, and over the removal of a number of loyal Chamberlainite Ministers to make room for these 'rebels'.

That much is common knowledge, but Einzig – who daily watched the Commons debates from the Gallery – believed that

> most Conservative Members felt, moreover, that any demonstration of their support to the new PM would be disloyal to his predecessor owing to the circumstances in which the change of Government came about ... they demonstrated their resentment by their sullen silence whenever Churchill entered the Chamber or rose to make a speech. This negative attitude became even more strikingly evident whenever Churchill sat down after concluding one of his historic speeches ... most Tory backbenchers remained sitting and silent.

Einzig also thought that this attitude had 'led many influential Americans to the conclusion that the Tory majority was not behind Churchill in his determination to fight on against heavy odds'.

Einzig told Chamberlain of these suspicions, adding that at least one foreign correspondent believed that the Tory behaviour constituted nothing less than 'a deliberate and organised demonstration against the Prime Minister'. He concluded: 'I know for a fact that on more than one occasion several ambassadors and important press correspondents left the House under the impression that the PM could not rely on the support of the Conservative majority.' Chamberlain replied to this letter, naturally denying that there was any 'want of loyalty to the Prime Minister among the Conservative backbenchers', but tacitly admitting that 'at the present time they are very deeply impressed with the gravity of the situation and they are in no mood to make extravagant demonstrations of any kind'. He went on to assure Einzig of 'my determination not to tolerate anything in the nature of half-hearted support'. More significantly, he told the correspondent that he would 'undertake to see that your impression is not confirmed by anything more serious'.

When a couple of days later, on 4 July, Churchill announced that the Vichy Fleet had been sunk by the Royal Navy at Oran, the Whips had been at work and, when he sat down, according to Einzig,

something remarkable happened. The Chief Whip, Margesson, rose to his feet. Turning towards the Tory backbenchers, he waved his Order Papers in a gesture clearly conveying that they too should rise. At his signal all the Conservatives, behind the Treasury bench and below the gangway ... rose to a man and burst into enthusiastic cheering at the top of their voices.

Churchill wept. Einzig was convinced that this demonstration of support was orchestrated, as only the day before in the Commons the Tories had 'pointedly cold-shouldered' the Prime Minister.

Einzig was perhaps playing down the drama and intense sense of relief of the occasion, whilst over-emphasizing his own role in alerting Chamberlain to the problem, but, 'On the evidence of my own eyes and several of my colleagues – all trained observers of Parliamentary proceedings and forewarned by me what to look out for – with whom I compared notes immediately after the scene, I am satisfied without a shadow of a doubt that ... the Tory change was not spontaneous.' He believed that it was 'unquestionable that the Tories had risen to cheer Churchill some seconds after Labour' in response to a signal by Margesson. This incident bore all the signs of Chamberlain asking his 'friends', via Margesson, to be more overt in their support of his successor as Prime Minister.

In his war memoirs, Churchill certainly considered that speech a watershed in his relations with the Tory Party. He reminisced how

the House was very silent during the recital but at the end there occurred a scene unique in my own experience. Everybody seemed to stand up all round, cheering, for what seemed a long time. Up till this moment the Conservative Party had treated me with some reserve and it was from the Labour benches that I received the warmest welcome when I entered the House or rose on serious occasions. But now all joined in solemn stentorian accord.

One historian of the Churchill Government believes that the Oran demonstration proved that the 'Conservatives had at last reconciled themselves to the coalition'. However, it seems that even that support had been stage-managed, and there were still serious doubts about Churchill on the benches behind him.

The same evening, Harry Crookshank dined at White's with Chamberlain's former Agriculture Minister, Sir Reginald Dorman-Smith. He recorded how Dorman-Smith was 'very worried about Home Defence. Had seen Winston whom he thought complacent and a lot of whiskies and soda.' Churchill's drinking was a regular gripe of Chamberlainites. 'I happened to meet [Field Marshal Sir] Philip Chetwode at luncheon,' Halifax wrote to Chamberlain at about this time, 'who led me aside and said, "Do stop Winston – he's drinking too much." You said you might have it in mind to say a word. Philip's evidence was quite good.' We may wonder whether their concern was wholly genuine, or part of the general air of moral superiority the Chamberlainites tended to affect towards Churchill.

On 6 July Beaverbrook explained to Hoare: 'The Government's standing with the public is not as it was. They are criticised in the newspapers over the use of manpower and a supposed lack of energy and direction in organising home defence.' Although he considered such criticism ill-founded, it 'reflects a general discontent'. Hoare also received a letter from his former PPS and devotee, John Moore-Brabazon, written on the same day. 'Between ourselves,' it began, 'Winston is getting more Chamberlain than Chamberlain and nobody, I understand, can approach him and nobody can say a word to him.'

Moore-Brabazon, who was sacked as Minister of Aircraft Production in 1942 after publicly making the very Chamberlainite observation that the Russo-German conflict 'suited us', was one of the first and very few to be critical of Churchill in the 1950s. In his autobiography he wrote that the meetings of the committee which co-ordinated the Battle of the Atlantic

> were the most unpleasant meetings I have ever attended ... the way Churchill treated everyone was almost unbearable. He usually appeared after his early afternoon sleep in the vilest of tempers.... He behaved as if he were a bullying schoolmaster. Everyone, in his opinion, was a halfwit; if anyone said anything he was jumped on and snubbed.

He finished by saying that Graham Sutherland's scathing portrait of the Prime Minister, which Lady Churchill later secretly destroyed, 'exactly portrays the man as he appeared to the committee whose unfortunate duty it was to attend'.

By the third week of July, criticism at last began to

lessen. Even the curmudgeonly Headlam described Churchill's radio broadcast of 14 July as 'less bombastic than usual and full of vim'. Waterhouse called the decision to send the Duke of Windsor to the Bahamas 'a much criticised Winstonianism', but supported the wide emergency powers that the Government took for itself in the case of invasion. He called the leading opponent of these measures, Sir Richard Acland, 'that miserable tapeworm' and considered that 'a little bit of Hitler's "just-a-po" [Gestapo], as Winston called it, would do them good'.

Butler better appreciated the power the Chamberlainites still wielded and wrote to Hoare: '[Labour War Cabinet member Arthur] Greenwood talks openly of the danger of alienating the Tory Party since they are the majority in the House.' Recalling the experience of the failed Davies/Amery attempted coup against Chamberlain, he added: 'If intrigues or attacks ... grow to any great extent all we have to do is pull the string of the toy dog of the 1922 Committee and make it bark. After a few staccato utterances it becomes clear that the Government depends upon the Tory squires for their majority.' If he had not become a politician, Rab would have made a fine political journalist.

Euan Wallace noted on 23 July that 'we are gradually moving back towards a Parliamentary opposition'. Kingsley Wood's budget that day, which had put a shilling on income tax and introduced a purchase tax, was unpopular with the Tory right. Waterhouse, however, was content with the general political situation, so long as Chamberlain and Halifax were there to restrain Churchill:

The three men who are at the head of affairs here today make a powerful combination. Edward Halifax deeply religious almost a mystic, not perhaps very practical-minded but a great moral strength; Neville Chamberlain not devout but certainly a man of high moral purpose and strong religious conviction, practical and analytic and above all clear-headed to a degree, and no less important capable of equally clear argument; Winston Churchill dynamic, explosive, brilliant in exposition and forceful in argument and I hope in action almost ruthless.

Churchill himself approved of this collective view of his Government, telling the *Manchester Guardian* journalist, W.P. Crozier, on 26 July how much he had liked an article which took this line. 'You see, after all,' he said, 'Chamberlain and those other people represent the Conservative Party which has a great majority in the House of Commons and they must be shown some consideration.' He was, despite his popularity in the country, very alive to potential weakness in the event of continued military reverses. 'I owe something to Chamberlain, you know. When he resigned he could have advised the King to send for Halifax and he didn't.... Chamberlain works very well with me and I can tell you this – he's no intriguer.'

When at the end of July Churchill said that he wanted a foreign affairs debate conducted in secret session, no fewer than 109 MPs voted against his proposal. Party politics returned with a vengeance when, on the last day of the month, the 1922 Committee was shown a leaflet which had been circulating in Birmingham claiming that Government successes were due mainly to Labour ministers. 'Great indignation was expressed,' recorded Wallace. Headlam believed: 'There is of course a "Party truce" but it is only observed by one side. Every speech made by the Labour people in the House of Commons is a Party speech and is propaganda.' The unspoken criticism was that by continually emphasizing the national side of the coalition, Churchill was allowing a situation to develop in which, as Headlam put it, 'everything we ought to stand for will go by default'.

On 15 August 57 German planes were shot down. More than any other, that day allowed the country to glimpse victory in the Battle of Britain. Returning from Fighter Command HQ at Stanmore in north London, Churchill instructed Colville to telephone the good news to Chamberlain in the country, who was 'overcome with joy'. Yet even on that great day the politicians were disputing amongst themselves and against Churchill. An Independent MP, Austin Hopkinson, asked him why he refused to give details about the composition of Lord Swinton's new Home Defence (Security) Executive, which was designed to 'ensure action' was taken against fifth columnists. Hopkinson said that he objected to Swinton's 'activities on behalf of big business in politics' – which Waterhouse considered 'a clear charge of corruption'. An angry Prime Minister snapped back that, 'if my honourable friend had paid half the attention to the full and very respectful statement which I have made to the House that he was accustomed to obstructing my efforts to get this country properly defended before the War, I would not have to answer his question at all'. Hopkinson asked for the Speaker's protection from this 'gross and lying innuendo' and other Members cried 'withdraw' at the Prime Minister.

Churchill continued: 'Far from withdrawing what I said, I will take the liberty of sending him a copy of one of his interventions in Debate, which I looked up only last night, in which he did his utmost to discredit me when I was doing my utmost for the country.' Waterhouse thought a 'hit well below the belt', but Churchill 'had my sympathy – those who start free fights must expect as good, and, when W.C. is their antagonist, better than they give'. Hopkinson replied: 'I recently looked up the same thing myself and discovered that intervention fully justified up to the hilt.' The reference was to a speech of Hopkinson's on 21 May 1936, in which he accused Churchill of promoting air rearmament partly as an anti-Baldwin manoeuvre. One might have thought that, of all days, 15 August 1940 was an inauspicious day to bring up that particular *canard*.

According to Waterhouse, the House 'warmed to the fight, notably Hore-Belisha, [the Liberal MP Edgar] Granville and Clement Davies, with many Liberals and socialists against the P.M.'. The Labour MP, Ernest Thurtle, 'in due course piped up with the remark that many of those complaining most were lukewarm about the prosecution of the War'. Bevan, in a reply recorded by Waterhouse but not Hansard, called Thurtle a pimp:

Thurtle complained and asked for a withdrawal of this 'foul and offensive term', but the Speaker seems to have resigned himself to his fate of sitting in the House with liars and pimps, neither of which are apparently unparliamentary innuendoes, and merely said he thought 'it is time that this unedifying incident ceased'. The Prime Minister then got up and gave news of a defeat and retreat in Somaliland about which none of these noisy patriots seemed to care a damn.

The news that Churchill intended to give the United States ninety-nine-year leases on certain Caribbean and Newfoundland military bases went down very badly with the Tory imperialist right. The House was anyhow 'languid', which Colville put down to their not being used to sitting during August. Waterhouse 'did not like' the way 'in which news was prefaced by an assurance that of course there was no question of a cession – possibly a distinction but not a material difference'. On further consideration he was 'glad it had been done, sorry it had to be done'. Somerset de Chair agreed and was 'profoundly disturbed at his calmly handing our strategic bases to USA', reasoning that 'after three generations no American politician is going to give them back'. When he remonstrated with Churchill, he was told: 'I would sooner they had them than a lot of Wops. ... We cannot expect to hold everything.' A motion de Chair tabled to shorten the length of the leases was signed by a roll-call of the senior Chamberlainites on the Tory right: Lord Winterton, Sir Herbert Williams, the recently elected Major-General Sir

Frederick Sykes, Sir Ernest Graham-Little, Right Club member Lord Edmund Crichton-Stuart and John Stourton amongst them. No longer in the Government, Alan Lennox-Boyd was also able to sign.

Three days later Crozier interviewed Hore-Belisha, who told him that he 'was afraid that Churchill would be prevented' from reconstructing the Government according to merit, 'by the claims of the Tory Party machine and by the dictatorship exercised by Captain Margesson. It would be "monstrous" if the principle of party balance in the Government had to be so rigidly maintained that Churchill could not choose the best man for the jobs and this was now to be feared.' According to Crozier, Hore-Belisha 'clearly implied that Churchill would like to make certain appointments but could not do so, or was likely to be prevented from doing so, by Captain Margesson and the "machine" '. This could easily be written off as the self-serving explanation of a disappointed ex-minister, who could neither forgive nor forget his sacking at Chamberlain's hands eight months earlier. But the very next day Crozier saw Beaverbrook, who told him that the Prime Minister had 'wanted to bring Herbert Morrison into the War Cabinet recently but the Tory "machine" would not let him'.

The underlying fact is clear: even on the day that the Luftwaffe began its all-night raids on London, Churchill was constrained by the Tory hierarchy over whom he could or could not appoint to his War Cabinet. Far from halting their internecine feuding when the nation was in danger, the politicians went on with their jockeying and criticizing unabated. Churchill might have been forgiven for wondering what he could possibly do to win the unqualified support of his Party.

By early September rumours were circulating 'that Winston is going to lead the Tory Party and he will when in the saddle get rid of the Munich Men'. The evidence for this was the adoption of his son Randolph for the vacant Preston seat, as well as the now-public knowledge that Chamberlain was seriously ill. On 5 September Chips Channon wrote:

> In the House, Winston ... spoke at some length, but he was not at his best, and evoked little enthusiasm; the House has become accustomed to his high-flown rhetoric and thinks that he jokes too much: it is true that he is rarely serious about even sacred things, such as loss of life, and he betrays too easily how he is enjoying power.

Over the years politicians had become inured to Churchill's rhetoric in a way that ordinary radio listeners were not. Practised nit-pickers, they were the last group of people in the country to be overwhelmed by his personality and leadership.

Chamberlain's operation for cancer on 9 September convinced him that 'any ideas which may have been in my mind about possibilities of further political activity and even a possibility of another Premiership after the War have gone'. Nancy Dugdale was at the same time telling her husband that, although 'Winston is enormously popular', his coalition was 'definitely unpopular and I believe 45 that . . . the House of Commons is very out of gear'. Shakes Morrison, a Chamberlainite former minister, told her that 'the PM's star was waning' and Ernest Bevin was 'training to be the next PM'.

The resentment of the Chamberlainites died hard, and they made spirited and determined efforts to continue trying to see the May 1940 crisis in a traditional left/right context long after everyone else realized that the terms of reference in British politics had undergone a profound change. In September 1940 the Duke of Devonshire voiced his suspicion that before May, 'Herbert M[orrison] as near as possible as he could told the workers to slack till their leaders were taken into the Government'. When the news broke that Chamberlain had cancer, Channon's first thought was that 'the leadership of the Party must then become Rab's, if there is a Conservative Party'.

Churchill's speech at the next secret session had once again to wind up with a plea 'to the House to show its consideration to Ministers.... We really are doing our very best.... I ask therefore for the indulgence of the House and for its support in not requiring too many sittings in the next month or two.'

The Dakar fiasco, when British and Free French forces were humiliatingly repulsed from the Vichyite capital of French West Africa, provided a perfect opportunity for critics of the Prime Minister to emerge from the woodwork and attack him directly, something the exigencies of the national emergency had not allowed in the previous couple of months. The alacrity with which they grabbed it shows the depth of the latent hostility still felt by Chamberlainites towards him and his regime. Victor Cazalet noted how 'all Winston's bad characteristics are now coming out'. Headlam wrote: 'it all beats me, and the whole thing smells of Winston! An affair of this kind, unless it is a success, is worse than useless and decidedly bad for our prestige, if we still possess any of that commodity so far as our "planning" is concerned.' Patrick Hannon wrote to Churchill to say that, in his constituency, 'the feeling of criticism and resentment is acute. Frankly the Dakar retreat is regarded as a cardinal blunder: more grave and far-reaching than the recall of our expeditionary force from Norway.' He went so far as to record his 'suspicion that there is want of foresight and vision in high places'.

Channon wondered whether Dakar was 'just a Winstonian scheme in his earlier, rasher manner', and believed it 'revealed the PM to be as incautious as ever. It is a deplorable affair and feeling in the Carlton Club is running high against him'. Admiral Beamish thought that, in the House of Commons, Churchill 'managed to slide across the Dakar incident with some adroitness but many had doubts and I am confident a grave error has been made'. All this fulminating against what was, in the wider context of the war, merely a sideshow of a sideshow, shows how sceptical they still were about Churchill and how ready to criticize him, even in the month when Britain lost 160,000 tons of shipping and the Blitz was approaching its height.

The reshuffle following Chamberlain's resignation took place on 3 October, but could not be as extensive as Churchill wished, owing to Halifax's refusal to leave the Foreign Office. Churchill did bring Oliver Lyttelton from outside politics into the Presidency of the Board of Trade. When attempting to find a constituency, Lyttelton met Lord Windlesham, the Vice-Chairman of the Conservative Party, to discuss the vacant Wrekin seat. Windlesham asked him whether his candidature 'was backed by Winston' and, when he was told that it was, said Churchill's support was 'a great mistake but it can't be helped'. Bracken was furious when he heard about this, but the hierarchy of the voluntary side of the Party was almost uniformly Chamberlainite. The Party Treasurer, Lord Marchwood, had even considered refusing to continue in office when Chamberlain fell, until persuaded to by Margesson.

In October Lloyd George was disappointed not to be appointed to the Cabinet after his arch-enemy Chamberlain's departure, but consoled himself by confiding to his private secretary: 'I shall wait until Winston is bust.' It may have been about this time, too, that Baldwin reputedly told Cazalet: 'My time is not yet. It may come soon. At present I am low and Winston is high. Who knows how soon the positions may be reversed?' Certainly Channon, four days after recognizing that 'the Churchill regime will never offer me anything', went back on the offensive against the 'Glamour Boys'. According to him, 'now so prominent and powerful, after being fallow for so long, [they] are a makeshift and shoddy lot. Their only merit has been long subservience to Winston.'

On 8 October Randolph Churchill took his seat in the House. He was introduced by Margesson. Waterhouse felt that one would have expected it to be an occasion of a remarkable demonstration. In fact the remarkable circumstance was the absence of any enthusiasm. The affair was treated more as a joke than a rather triumphal moment in the P.M.'s life. But the House is that way inclined. Its opinions are not very consistent and I fear it will not be long before the acclamations which have cheered Winston the attacker and successor of the hated Neville will be heard no more when not Winston the rebel but Churchill the Conservative Party Leader faces the House. From his own point of view I think he has made a mistake.

Waterhouse was referring to Churchill's decision to accept the Leadership of the Conservative Party, given up by the dying Chamberlain. Far from being reconciled to Churchill by the time of the sinking of the French fleet in early July 1940, as most historians have suggested, the Tory Party was still suspicious of him. In October a man with his ear so close to the Tory ground as Waterhouse could remark that, 'Everyone realises the inevitability of the change ... but no one pretends to like it.' There had long been 'a simmering dislike of Churchill' in the 1922 Committee, and this resurfaced at their meeting held just before the leadership election in Caxton Hall, Westminster, which took place at 4.30 p.m. on 9 October. Beamish records how, at that meeting, 'some malcontents made the best they could of their promises to accept as our new leader the PM', considering Sir Archibald Southby, Sir Herbert Williams, Austin Hopkinson 'and some others' as people who 'professionally oppose the P.M.'.

Clementine Churchill did not want her husband to become Party Leader, but to remain instead a purely national figure. However, Beaverbrook and Bracken – using Lloyd George's fate in 1922 to show what happened to 'national' figures without party backing – made him see the sense of it. One does not turn down the leadership of the majority party lightly and Churchill knew that the Tories needed him as much as he them. Beaverbrook also 'pointed out the danger of divided loyalties, of possible complaints against Churchill by Conservative back-benchers' if anyone else was allowed to take Chamberlain's mantle. By taking on the Leadership, Churchill was paradoxically showing how politically weak he still perceived himself to be.

It was at this time that the young Chamberlainite MP, George Harvie-Watt, showed Churchill around his anti-aircraft unit stationed at Redhill. He remembered how

the PM started talking politics to me. There had been a meeting of the Conservative Party to elect a leader and there were some cliques in the Party who said that Churchill should not become leader and that he would be in a stronger position without too strong a Party attachment.... The PM asked me what I thought about these developments at Westminster. I said it would be fatal if he did not lead the Conservative Party.... He was still suspicious of them and of their attitude to him before the war. I said ... essentially he must have a majority and I was sure this majority could only come from the Conservative Party. He questioned me a lot about the strength of ministers and what influence they wielded. I replied that if you have a strong army of MPs under you, ministers could be won over or crushed, if necessary. He seemed to appreciate my arguments and thanked me very much.

Harvie-Watt little realized that he was being sounded out as a potential PPS for Churchill, precisely because of his Chamberlainite connections.

At the Caxton Hall meeting of the Conservative Party on 9 October Halifax took the chair, thanked Chamberlain and proposed Churchill as the new Leader. These were put together, in an 'omnibus' resolution, so that no Tory could vote in favour of the first and against the second, as Waterhouse suspected some Tory MPs would have liked. Just prior to leaving for the Hall, Halifax wrote to Lady Alexandra Metcalfe to say that he found his speech 'very difficult to do', but the next day he said he had been told that he 'had not put my foot in the rather boggy ground!' According to Crookshank, Halifax made 'a beautifully phrased speech', treading the careful line between praise for the two men. Beamish noted how he 'paid a wonderful tribute to Mr Chamberlain who was not present, very firmly and in fine language he praised Neville C. for his efforts to keep peace and gain time ... to overcome the madness of our people in their almost criminal unreadiness for inevitable war'.

He then spoke for a much shorter period about Churchill, and eventually put the resolution to the vote. In the national emergency, let alone the absence of alternative candidates, it is hardly surprising that nobody actually voted against. Instead, the electoral college, consisting of Tory MPs, peers in receipt of the Conservative Whip and Executive Committee members of the National Union, elected Churchill *nemine contradictente*. This, as Beamish pointed out, was not the same as unanimously, because it meant 'that some did not vote for or against, but they were few'.

Churchill then entered the Hall to 'a good but not tempestuous welcome'. He gave 'a good speech of acceptance', lasting about ten minutes and, in Wallace's opinion, 'hitting exactly the right note as usual'. He certainly hit a right-wing note, concentrating on those subjects – the Empire, the left-wing threat and so on – most likely to appeal to Chamberlainites. Indeed, as he had put it in rather different circumstances three decades earlier, he served up 'sentiment by the bucketful, patriotism by the Imperial pint'. He naturally paid an extravagant tribute to his predecessor, emphasizing 'how close had been his work' with Chamberlain over the previous thirteen months, and how their 'friendship had grown'. He then dealt frankly with Tory concerns about his personality, chaffing himself 'gently about his alleged fickleness'. For a speech of acceptance for the leadership of a party on which he had 'ratted' and 're-ratted', it was a masterpiece.

The extent to which he was willing to appease the Tory right can be perceived from the statement that 'his basic belief in and support of the imperial outlook was his main incentive to accept the leadership'. After that 'he stressed the importance of speaking with authority on behalf of the Party and the organisation in the Cabinet'.

Yet not everyone was impressed. Beamish sat next to the Chamberlainite MP, Sir John Power, who 'blamed [Churchill's] Ten-Year Rule' for British military unpreparedness, and when leaving the Hall, Kenneth Pickthorn told him that Churchill was 'a word-spinner, a second-rate rhetorician'. Pickthorn's son remembers how his father 'thought Churchill's judgment fearful. Right to the end he thought him a disastrous war leader, albeit a vigorous personality. He thought Churchill pretty invariably chose the wrong course of action.' Halifax wrote to Chamberlain after the meeting that he had been touched by the 'evident personal feeling of real sorrow and regret and regard for you. Nor was there any doubt as to the overwhelming sense of the meeting as to what you had done to keep the peace of the world as long as you could.'

When Channon met Churchill in the House the day after the Caxton Hall meeting, he wondered 'why he always bows and withdraws into himself when he is aware of hostility ... he seems to contract, suddenly to look smaller and his famous charm is overclouded by an angry taurine look'. Churchill was, for all his Olympian efforts, leading a party which was still at soul Chamberlainite.

On 11 November 1940 the Royal Navy attacked and crippled the Italian fleet at Taranto. Much relieved, Churchill told Channon before announcing the news in the Commons that 'we have some sugar for the birds this time'. Perhaps it was their flightiness and twittering that led him to choose that metaphor for his backbenchers. 53

The news won him little respite. Only two days later Lord Kemsley, the Chairman of Allied Newspapers and Editor-in-Chief of the *Sunday Times*, told Woolton that 'people have become very critical of Churchill: whilst fully recognising that he represented the spirit of the nation and made marvellous speeches, they were beginning to doubt the quality of the government – in which, of course they are quite right'. The newspaper magnate went on to surmise that, 'if there had been an Opposition, the government would have gone over Dakar, but the whole trouble was that there was no alternative P.M'.

On 12 November the Commons heard Churchill's panegyric on Chamberlain, who had died three days before. Beamish uncharitably considered it 'flawless as a rhetorical effort, but a close examination reveals a clear intention to make the late P.M. shoulder the blame for what has happened and to buttress his own efforts past and present'. He thought Churchill employed 'deliberate faint praise', and concluded: 'no wonder some men distrust the P.M. for his capacity for cajolery and fervent persuasive English'. Churchill had been fortunate, felt Beamish: he 'became P.M. at a very perfect moment. I incline to the feeling that had Churchill been P.M. in 1938 or before we should have slid into war unprepared or disunited.' Of Chamberlain he thought: 'it takes a great-hearted man to accept with perfect loyalty service under a man such as Churchill when he has been the cause of your downfall'. This was the rewriting of history on a grand scale.

The funeral at Westminster Abbey on 14 November 1940 was an emotional experience for Chamberlainites.

Waterhouse was 'sick to see the solemn humbugging expressions on the faces of some of those who had made his last months a hell'. Colville 'noticed the look of blank indifference, almost of disdain, on Duff Cooper's face, the boredom of Bevin. Only Anderson and Hankey sang the hymns.' Channon felt that 'some seemed to be gloating', but admitted that 'Winston ... had the decency to cry', which was not in itself perhaps too much of a tribute from the most lachrymose Prime Minister since Lord Goderich. There were many occasions when Churchillian tears were shed during the war, but none were more politically felicitous than these.

In stark contrast to the rock-solid national belief in victory, the House of Commons was less certain. On 19 November Morris-Jones noted in his diary that 'several Members consider that we cannot get a victory over Germany, that the best we can expect is a stalemate'. It may have been the British people's 'Finest Hour', but the same cannot be said for the politicians.

Woolton wrote in his diary on 20 November 1940:

> Chamberlain succeeded in getting a personal allegiance from members of his government, because although he was not strong he was absolutely reliable and trustworthy. There is no allegiance to Churchill; there is nobody in the government whom the public would trust.

By late November criticisms were not coming solely from Chamberlainites such as Cazalet; on the 28th even the Liberal MP, Clement Davies, was complaining to his fellow Welshman Lloyd George that 'the government had a really bad time yesterday ... the House was seething.... I am afraid Winston is so absorbed in playing the part of Marlborough, Nelson and Trenchard that he has no time for the more mundane things. Last night Members came to ask me to put down a motion for radical reconstruction.'

February 1941 saw yet another spat between the Prime Minister and the Chamberlainites, this time over Churchill's practice of sending potential political opponents abroad. Churchill, who had joked of Horace Wilson that 'if he comes [to No. 10] any more ... I'll make him Governor of Greenland!', had sent Halifax into exile two months earlier.

Churchill wanted, as Baffy Dugdale put it, to have the National Labour MP and Chamberlainite minister, Malcolm MacDonald, 'banished to Canada' as High Commissioner. Beverley Baxter told Hoare in Madrid that he found the appointment 'astonishing ... the general feeling is that now the official Labour Party is supporting Winston, he wants to liquidate the National Labour platoon altogether'. Baxter, acknowledging that 'Churchill and Beaverbrook have no love for the Conservative Party', said that before he died the Colonial Secretary, Lord Lloyd, had feared that Churchill and Beaverbrook might form 'a new central party' with Bevin, and as a result 'he was very anxious about the future of the Conservative Party.'

In order to allow MacDonald to continue as an MP, legislation had to be introduced which would permit the Executive to issue certificates which would override the normal rules of disqualification for MPs accepting 'offices of profit under the Crown'. Chamberlainites both spoke and voted against the Disqualification (Temporary Provisions) Bill on its Second Reading. Although the main opponents came from the 'awkward squad', Kenneth Pickthorn, Lord Winterton and Austin Hopkinson, it was the Independent Labour Party MP, John McGovern, who put the case most bluntly, warning that the measure would help Churchill 'create around himself a servile force, making Parliament a paid institution to keep the Government and Prime Minister in office'. Many Chamberlainites agreed that this process would only be aggravated by a Bill which allowed MacDonald to be, in Waterhouse's characteristically direct phrase, 'kicked out'. During the debate on 27 February, Churchill's speech was interrupted. According to Headlam, 'Winston is apparently very angry with some of us for venturing to criticise his measure which is being introduced in order to enable Winston to get rid of young MacDonald (or anyone else) . . .'

By declaring that he regarded the vote on the measure as one of confidence in his ministry, Churchill displayed, in Headlam's opinion, 'a very childish exhibition of temper'. MacDonald, the son of the former Prime Minister, was deluged with letters from friends disapproving the move, all more or less along the lines of one which read: 'this Government can ill afford to lose you, one of the few people [we] genuinely trust. It looks as if none but "yes" men are wanted!' From Washington Lord Halifax noted 'the feeling' among political *cognoscenti* 'about Winston sending Malcolm to Ottawa. I deprecated it when Winston first mentioned the idea. He doesn't think much of him – He's wrong; but he's not at all Winston's type! (Any more than I am!)' Over both the cession of the Irish Treaty ports in 1938 and the Palestine White Paper in 1939 Churchill had vigorously opposed policies MacDonald had championed.

A Select Committee was appointed under Sir Dennis Herbert, the Conservative Deputy Speaker and Chairman of the Ways and Means Committee, to examine the whole question of disqualification. His report turned out to be so complex that the Government was able to ignore its recommendations. With Hoare in Madrid, Halifax in Washington and MacDonald in Ottawa the scene was set for a number of other such banishments. Chamberlain's former Agriculture Minister, Sir Reginald Dorman-Smith, was sent out to govern Burma as soon as the legislation was passed; later in the war Churchill sent Lord Swinton off to be Minister Resident in West Africa and, much against his will, John Colville to be Governor of Bombay.

Churchill's attempt to exile his noisiest and most persistent critic in the Party, the Tory MP for Horsham, Lord Winterton, failed, however. The holder of an Irish peerage, Winterton was not debarred from sitting in the House of Commons. He refused the Governor-Generalship of South Africa in February 1941, despite Churchill telling him, 'It is a wonderful climate, you can sleep outside under a wagon any time.' Instead, in Headlam's words, the rebel 'plugs away at the idea of forming an alternative national Government'.

As Churchill had predicted, Britain entered 'great

dangers and great trials' in April 1941. The decision to send 60,000 troops to Greece had the Chamberlainite MP, Jay Llewellin, telling Beaverbrook, as he was going off to attend a War Cabinet: 'Remember three words: Gallipoli – Narvik – Dunkirk.' Sure enough, when the army had to be evacuated soon after it had landed, Churchill's critics promptly re-emerged. Wavell evacuated Benghazi on the 7th, Coventry was blitzed the next day and on the 20th Rommel attacked Tobruk. It was a black period, but rather than displaying self-discipline and at last giving Churchill the national unity he needed – and after eleven months of leadership surely had a right to expect – Chamberlainites and others instead heaped criticism on him and his Government.

Beamish attended an informal meeting of senior Chamberlainite backbenchers on 23 April (St George's Day), after the evacuation of Greece had been ordered. Among others there were present Colonel Edward Wickham (Margesson's PPS), Malcolm McCorquodale, Sir Douglas Thomson (PPS to Ronald Cross), Sir George Davies, Sir Percy Hurd and Sir Malcolm Robertson, all but the last of whom had voted for Chamberlain at the Norway debate. They expressed 'the same anxiety' over 'the bad patch'. They spoke of 'if we pull through' and 'if we win'. Hore-Belisha leapt at the opportunity to bring up the old canard of the Prime Minister's drinking, telling Morris-Jones that he 'regards the P.M. as a danger. He says he has no judgment and predicts when some calamity will arise as a result of his change of strategy. He lunched with the P.M. today; plum pudding mixed with wine and later brandy. P.M. took him to his deep dug-out which was full of whisky bottles, etc!'

A motion of 'no confidence' in Churchill's Government was called for 7 May 1941, where there were, in Beamish's phrase, 'the usual speeches by ex-Ministers who had been tried and found wanting and a few wanting to be tried, some who are very trying and still others who might almost be described as wanting'. Lloyd George and Hore-Belisha led the attack, which only served to solidify Tory support for Churchill. Beamish's dislike of Hore-Belisha ('a potent and pungent Jew') seems to have been primarily on racial grounds. He also described the Government's Labour critic, Emanuel Shinwell, as 'a clever poisonous Socialist Polish Jew ... very far from an honest man and an Englishman.'

During the debate Channon thought that 'Winston looked uncomfortable.' Harold Nicolson was happier: 'Members are a bit defeatist. But Winston cheers them up. Yesterday it was rather like a hen-coop of wet hens: today they all strutted like bantams.' Beaverbrook believed that whilst there were 'no politics at home, it is true that there are still politicians with their ambitions and rivalries'. Clearly no national danger was too great for these to be indulged to the full. Although hardly any MPs actually voted for the motion, Waterhouse thought

> the House in a very fractious mood. Ready to find fault at every turn. Hore-Belisha, Shinwell, Winterton, each with small groups about them, Herbert Williams, Archie Southby and others of our friends are restive. Erskine-

Hill and what he calls 'the boys', by which he means his 1922 Committee Executive, are extremely active.

The difference between the rock-solid allegiance of the nation and the intrigues, cabalism and disloyalty of the politicians could not have been more marked.

The German invasion of Crete on 20 May 1941, followed by the British evacuation within eleven days, led the diplomat, Oliver Harvey, to write to the anti-appeasement Tory MP, Paul Emrys-Evans, that Churchill must take the blame, and if he fell there were only Lloyd George and Beaverbrook to take his place. Channon recorded how 'on all sides one hears increasing criticism of Churchill. He is undergoing a noticeable slump in popularity and many of his enemies, long silenced by his personal popularity, are once more vocal. Crete has been a great blow to him.'

The long guerrilla warfare between Churchillians and Chamberlainites had finally ended in July 1941 in victory for the former. No national crisis had proved so perilous as to silence the mutterings and moans of the dispossessed group. When the nation outside Parliament unified to meet the Nazi threat, imposing upon itself an extraordinary self-discipline, their elected representatives schemed, criticized and joined cabals to withhold full-hearted support from the coalition. This phenomenon was perfectly summed up by Channon, who, after the 'no confidence' motion of 6 May 1941, 'despaired of England and of democracy all day, and yet I seldom enjoyed a day more, thanks to the intrigues'.

Apart from those few months in the summer of 1940 when the British people expected invasion daily, Parliamentary cabals became more outspoken as the military situation became more desperate. Some may consider these mutterings – which were rarely heard far beyond the Palace of Westminster – as an encouraging sign that Britain remained a functioning pluralist democracy even in her darkest hour. But, despite Colville's assertion that after fourteen days of Churchill's leadership the Establishment had coalesced behind Churchill, it is clear that the Respectable Tendency actually spent fourteen months putting Party before country, and love of intrigue before both.